Marie-Louise Eyres

Fish, Salt, Blood, and Inkings

SurVision Books

First published in 2025 by
SurVision Books
Dublin, Ireland
Reggio di Calabria, Italy
www.survisionmagazine.com

Copyright © Marie-Louise Eyres, 2025

Cover art: Rose Farshad, *Untitled.* Courtesy of the artist.
Copyright © Rose Farshad, 2025

Design © SurVision Books, 2025

ISBN: 978-1-912963-63-8

This book is in copyright. No part of this publication may be reproduced, stored in a retrieval system, or transmitted in any form or by any means without the prior permission in writing from the publisher. The book is sold subject to the condition that it shall not, by way of trade or otherwise, be lent, resold or otherwise circulated without the publisher's prior consent in any form of binding or cover other than that in which it is published and without a similar condition, including this condition, being imposed on the subsequent purchaser.

NO AI TRAINING: Without in any way limiting the author's [and publisher's] exclusive rights under copyright, any use of this publication to "train" generative artificial intelligence (AI) technologies to generate text is expressly prohibited.

Acknowledgments

Grateful acknowledgment is made to the editors of the following, in which some of these poems, or versions of them, originally appeared:

Alchemy Spoon: "Widow"

Alien Buddha Zine: "The Peppers Are Weeping"

The Black Cat Nature Anthology: "The Green Man"

Bridport Prize Anthology 2025: "Rules of Wolf "

Broken Spine Press: "Home"

Candlestick Press Almanac 2025: "May"

Candlestick Press Christmas Walks: "A Snow Cento"

DataBleedZine: "My Angels Are Orange"

HNDL Magazine: "Undercover in the City"

The Poetry Bus: "Snowshoe Hares" and "Incubatus"

The Poet's Republic: "Last Photo of My Dad Rowing on the River Thames"

PulseBeat Poetry: "Angel"

Shearsman Magazine: "Symbiosis"

Stand Magazine: "Loss Is an Egg"

A Snow Cento includes lines from Philip Larkin's *A Girl in Winter Snow*, as well as from poems by Louis MacNeice, Hardie St. Martin, Anna Akhmatova, and Paul Petrie.

CONTENTS

Loss Is an Egg	5
Angel	6
Creature, Maquette	7
Aftermath	8
I Am Feathered	9
My Angels Are Orange	10
Circle Dance, Chain Dance	11
Corpse Flower	12
In the Future	13
Undercover in the City	14
The Peppers Are Weeping	15
Snowshoe Hares	16
Incubatus	17
Widow	18
Last Photo of My Dad	19
House Burial	20
May	21
Rules of Wolf	22
Carpenter Bee	23
The Green Man	24
Home	25
Rainstorm in the Masai Mara	26
First Winter in Santa Monica	27
A Snow Cento	28
Reincarnation	29
Symbiosis	30

Loss Is an Egg

Loss is a large, egg-shaped dip left in the bed.
It's a painted star that shined with sweat
all night upon a dancer's cheek.

It's the time you found that precious lock
of thick, dark curly hair
you'd clipped and twined, before he shaved his head.

Loss lurks behind a satin eyepatch
that's masquerading as a prop, while hiding
an uncontrolled, diplopic eye.

And it's the place where onion grass
and tomatoes start to grow, making a scented salad
of the lawn, and the world shrinks

to one tight, well-trod suburban mile
where deer leave cloven prints in snow, two thumbs,
two thumbs again, across the stone-path leading to your house.

Loss is the casual gesture of a wrist, as you wipe
bath-steam from mirrors, mark time passing
every night, yes, every night.

Angel

I wish I'd had that angel fish inked
onto my shoulder blade, in my twenties
when I most longed for it. My artist wore double
denim and a handlebar mustache. And in his honeyed
drawl, he talked color options as seductively
as any man holding a sharp needle could. But
it would be faded now, just a blurry shadow-fish,
streaks of paling greens despite his steady hand.
Old fish dry out, scaled skin peels and itches flake,
all wash out with sun and salt along the ocean coast.
Yet when I look, I find this ink again
on curling papers pinned to tattoo-shop walls
beside bright orange carp, red octopus, rose-tangled
skulls, all waiting to be drawn on someone new.

Creature, Maquette

(after the sculpture by Lygia Clark)

I am a cacophony of hinges, polished nickel plates
swings and roundabouts, doors that open
further doors.

I am a broken flying thing
that never got off the ground. Peel my sides gently
like a tin of cat food when you're trying
not to slice your hands.

I have flickety switches, castanets, I'm the silver coin
you spin, moth-like across the bar

the latch of a window clasp, the church key
that opens a bottle of ale.

Maybe I'm just a flattened metal mouse, a retired puppet
or dragon's pointed snout. Wait no

I am the Sydney Opera House.

Aftermath

I got up only to fall, bite
into the ground. My thoughts scattered

like crickets, returned as soggy
whitewashed lemons.

I held my chin in my trembling fingers
the pressure inside my head a huge

black-knotted tree, while rain gathered
in small swamps and prehistoric marshes

among my sleeves. I couldn't eat
a spoonful of raw honey though

my throat was full of aching
grieving beauty, the frothy odor

of hawthorn & plum blossoms.
This was my hour of change.

I Am Feathered

Rows of black lashes sprout
from folds of blue nylon curtains
dressing the edges of this tiny room
like frilled cupcake papers.

The bed blooms with sweetness
it reeks of my blood, meds, high-sugar-skin.

And I am centered in it
like some plucked, monstrous poultry.

In sleep, there is a rustling of long
golden grasses.

Plums and apples tumble over dry ground
as fast unseen dogs
pursue them
panting.

My Angels Are Orange

When red hums along the edges of my tongue
like the buzz of cicada song, red may run out
streaking my chin. When indigo brushes
my shoulder blades, like a length of silky
nylon, borrowed hair, it moves with the light -
skin, indigo, skin.

When blue pierces my flesh, needlepoint & quick
blue is a quartet playing short, sharp strings
and green gurgles inside my gut. Then if green
is sour, a twisted steeple or copper ruin
so yellow promises sweetness, syruped peaches
yellow, high-blood-sugar skin. And orange sings its *O*
like a chorus of angels, *O, O, O!* of high and low
with dark pointy shoes and bright orange wings.

Circle Dance, Chain Dance

We trail the fringes of our shawls and coattails
through mustard seed and soft wet mud,
along the edges of the ebb tide,
colored like blackberry and cornflowers.
We carry the blood of lost children, ancestral blood,
beets and vinegars, precious dark cherries.
We spin like Botticelli's Graces,
the two circles of the Agahu dance,
the Hora, the Kolo, the Dabke.
We dance braid to braid,
hem to hem, and fingertip to shoulder bone.
Our feet are the drum, our knees are the drum,
our hips are the drum,
our breath is the drum, our hearts are the drum.

We are the drum.

Corpse Flower

oh, foul wafting pork chops, body parts
shank, hip, glute.

From crisping, purpled edges
into blackened cabbage.

Folks gather at garden displays
while the homeless hunker

around tin drum fires
under tarps of leaky plastics

reeking their own stinks,
& the man with a hacky sack face

lurks, always turning,
turning, to ask me something

about radicchio leaves
sutured with rotten meat.

In the Future

(after Italo Calvino)

The man shopping in the frozen aisle
without his right auricle will say *It was lost in the war
I tried wearing a wax one, but it kept...*

And the blind man on the curb
will tap my crutches with his white stick.

Street vendors will burn fires of cherrywood
sprinkled with sweet marjoram. An old man will sit
on the dock mending nets. He handles barnacles and sturgeon roe
as knots measure out his years.

All tattoos will fade. The little lizard on your arm
with red darting eyes, mutates into a tadpole.

I will be the meat in the hug sandwich
I will ride the shopping cart fast through the streets
my prize, one whipped raspberry mousse with a silver foil lid.

Undercover in the City

The night we watched the remake of *Total Recall*
I must have had one glass too many
coz I dreamt myself into the dark,
concrete world of neon signs & overcast skies,
right into a menaced tower block of crime.
I was on Earth with Colin Farrell
post apocalypse. Bullets shot past us, we took cover
inside a circus tent, bouquets exploded,
throwing out a stack of disembodied feet –
non-matching pairs that simply   float.
We did somersaults across a roof strung with fresh laundry
We swathed towels around our heads, damp turbans
suppressing any brain-implanted chips.
Just me and Colin Farrell running, leaping through the streets.

The Peppers Are Weeping

they'd hoped to hang, bulb-like
and blind to the outside world

sweetening with time
they'd slowly shrivel

lose their grip on the branch
but instead, the peppers

are weeping, gasping
breathless, their tiny seed teeth

hang tentatively
in quivering mouths

they did not expect to be sliced open
so early, some teeth

were knocked out
by the force of the knife.

Snowshoe Hares

Entice us with flame-darkened corn cob,
browned apple. Snare one long, ankle bone

with wire loop on a slender twig, choke us
'til we're dead. Be agile, swift in killing.

We offer acorn-colored lean-cuts
when deftly skinned of thick, white fur.

But remember, harvest us only
in winter months and be grateful

for this bread and butter. Deliver us
wrapped in fresh, wax paper,

each with our head chopped off.
The lady of the house does not like

to cook a coddle* with any creature
resembling her own, sleeping babes.

*coddle is an Irish stew made of game and vegetables.

Incubatus

Our house is a sleeping, multi-pocketed marsupial.
Crab-apples dangle outside.

Tucked in its hidden pouches
we each ferment like old blue cheeses,

like sulfates gathered in the silt
of bottled, mediocre wines.

Windowsills buckle with condensation,
puddling under sailboats of glass and lead.

This is a creature with rheumatic
joints, curled into the damp.

Not a place for storing cookbooks,
old polaroids and leather brogues,

without the bruise-like vines of mildew
creeping across them all.

But it never stirs this house, it sleeps,
dreamless and constant, couvade.

Widow

Winter light casts low across the empty
polished hall. Dressed in mourning and poised
to leave, her sleeves hide fading bruises
wreathed about her wrists. She knows black weeds
will cede to paler greys then purple silks
surrendering to cotton whites in time
for butter-melting August days
a salty breeze, soft dunes beside the sea. And yet
these well-walked rooms stand stiff with old
familiar creaks, a boreal iron stove
the scent of pork and peas, candlewax and bleach.
Wool rugs have been rolled up and then removed.
Echoes of raised voices, broken pots
and vows, fall silent now in death.

Last Photo of My Dad Rowing on the River Thames

He's front seat in a double scull, the spoons
of blades submerged, strong legs, knees bent, chin up.
The looms of oars point back like wings about
to launch. This late June sky is overcast
he grips the oars, with steely upward glance
that says *I must push on.* The faulty wiring
of his heart's already tripped, he'd fallen
on a run, then bled against the asphalt
in the dark. He capsized weeks before
this photograph was shot, laughed off the biting
chill of murky Thames. On Sunday he's forecast
to row but dies instead, with fleeting thoughts
of what, we wonder – copper beeches
muddy riverbank, perhaps us, cheering on.

House Burial

First time we tried to bury the house in sand,
tide washed it away,
spin drift,
it returned with burnished edges,
clam shells the size of fishing boats,
water rides and spigots sprouting from the roof.

Second time we tried to bury the house in palm leaves,
wind blew it away,
tumbleweed,
it returned with windows broken, over-run
with termites, sugar-beet root aphids
nibbling on the beams.

The last time we tried to bury the house in garbage,
rats carried it away,
cats feasted,
it returned festering, stinking like death,
sunflowers and tomato plants
blooming in its heat.

May

May is more than mud remains, the aftermath
of April's showers. It's a sudden burst
of uncontrolled, sharp, thistle-weeds
tomatoes sending feelers out
to find the heat. May is summer's blueprint
it sits above the squirrel-nested spruce
quivering on a top branch, needle fresh.
It hides in gutters along rooftops
then peeks through leaf-grates
fungi slim. It leaves flourishes of crabgrass
behind the bins, germinates in asphalt
softened by the sun. Its stalks are strong
as sundials, and some have tasseled shanks
that in later months, grow silky ears of corn.

Rules of Wolf

(after John Phillip Johnson)

Offal is beautiful. Breed as soon as you get the chance
and vomit for your young. You've only got six, maybe eight
winters if you stay wild, so be on your toes. Play the long game,
it pays to be beta, keep close to the ground, pack rules.
You were born endangered, mythologized, feared,
there's nothing you can change here. A sanctuary may take you in
where you'll survive for decades, even when you've lost the will to live,
are going deaf, stiff-hipped, loping along the same worn path of grass,
over and over, (it will only make them doubt your sanity).
Visiting hours will bring all the scents of rank behinds. No, you
won't get a chance to eat them. Just sleep behind their fences,
set off a group howl, they'll pay in venison for a tuneless chorus.
And when it's time for the needle, go quietly, look into their eyes,
appear to read their souls, let them believe they've been humane.

Carpenter Bee

Carpenter bees like wolf spiders
are solitary workers

without webs or colonies
they build their nests and leave.

Don't worry you won't be stung
by any bee today. Bone-weary

she has rasped her mandibles
against a tree, carved tunnels

into deadwood, laid her eggs.
Can you hear her larvae humming?

She cannot lull them now.
The bee brood tastes like peanuts

they are soft fodder to the woodpecker
who is nearby and always listens for her food.

The Green Man

I buried myself
in cabbage leaves,
to cool away from the sun,
to calm my heart-blood
and give salve to ulcers
that'd ravaged
the land of my skin.
And the thorns of the blackberry
twisted round
to shield me from beasts
of the hunt. While a bumblebee hid,
snug, soft by my ear
as she swapped her buzz
for a kiss.

Home

It was leaving the farm in the rain
I remember the most
not the glow of sunset across metal roofs
making magenta of day's end

or the silence of empty silos.

Barn windows held no reflection of sunnier days
gone was the thin scent of sourdough.

Dirt worked its way into wood
where paint had cracked deep
and rough, like layers of skin.

Prints in the mud from boots
and the half-lame dog
who never left his side

all washed away.

Rainstorm in the Masai Mara

In the Kenya plains outside our row of canvas tents
red earth has cracked into tile-size slabs.
An elephant strides across the barren water hole
swinging his empty trunk in search of something damp
to throw across his dusty back. We hold our precious rations
poured out in plastic cups, face the daily choice of drink or wash.

And as we gulp it down, large wet drops
fall earthbound for the first time in half a year
a smattering of great water marbles takes us
by surprise, makes us jump.

We squeeze shampoo onto mud-tangled hair
wash our mucky faces, arms, and legs
as the laterite clay streaks down our skin
back into the ground like long forgotten blood.

First Winter in Santa Monica

The bungalow smells of sun-warmed wood, the sea
a sour mix, fish taco, swilled brine, the sting of
dried salt. Grains of sand edge around
in cracks between dark boards of bath
and bedroom floors, critter traps balance
on shelves beside wash-soap
high above dark droppings. For five days
it rains biblically, kids jump in muddy backyard
puddles, the kitchen cacti bloom, little shocks
of pink among short needles. But not another drop
falls for a whole twelve months, maybe eighteen
and when rain finally breaks, the youngest child
holds out her hands – *what is this wet stuff*
falling from the sky?

A Snow Cento

There was no more snow during the night
frost on the great bay-window spawns snow and pink roses
the wind blows Niagara rainbows of snow over the city
where they wear galoshes to their armpits year-round.
It lays in ditches and in hollows, one vast shell. Upon the hard crest
of a snowdrift we tread, heads tossed back in song, and on ripe lips
catch the perfect flakes. Sunlight is too gold, the snow half gracious
fruitful, silver-quick, looping air like birds to broken bones
knotting rags of it on the limbs of trees. To look at the snow
too long has a hypnotic effect, cold seems to cramp the bones
candles have to be lit, ice in the jugs smashed. The long sword
of the frozen river shines. There's a slight silver chink of your spurs.
And after dark, elms all apple bloom at the backs of houses
where light shows around the edges of curtains.

Reincarnation

Next time, I'll not charge through life
I'll be a reindeer, stoic, portrait-still. As caribou
I'll not grieve the shed of velvet from my bones
antlers and a double coat
like fresh-shucked harvest corn will fall
each year.

Summer's amber eyes will slow-mutate
in time for winter months, to match the sky's blue hour.
And when I'm hunted, let me be butchered well
make of me blood sausages
a feast for the hunter's team.

Then stretch my new-cleaned skins with creases taut
across horse-run carioles and ride,
ride on.

Symbiosis

As this box of woven willow-grass rots down
cold flesh, all blood dried up, gone dark
shall blend with brown gypsum, red hematite.

When reaching under-forests, sprawling threads
I'll join the colonies of lion's mane
pale skinned milk-tooth, fast growing finger paths of light
among black trumpets.

And buried deep past hungry worms,
I'll mimic fungal symbiosis
at tips of Jacarandas across the California hills
offer nitrogen in fair exchange
for sugar from tree root.

Then I may just bear witness
to each subsequent spring bloom, the bee dances
swift ruby-throated hummingbirds on the dip
monarch butterflies stringing the heights of twisty
purple ferns.

Courtesy of mushroom, life shifts
mycologically from cell to tube to petal.
In the shade of indigo trees, violet has mixed
with curd white bone.

Selected Poetry Titles Published by SurVision Books

Contemporary Tangential Surrealist Poetry: An Anthology
Edited by Tony Kitt
ISBN 978-1-912963-44-7

Invasion: An Anthology of Ukrainian Poetry about the War
Edited by Tony Kitt
ISBN 978-1-912963-32-4

Noelle Kocot. *Humanity*
(New Poetics: USA)
ISBN 978-1-9995903-0-7

Helen Ivory. *Maps of the Abandoned City*
(New Poetics: England)
ISBN 978-1-912963-04-1

Tony Kitt. *The Magic Phlute*
(New Poetics: Ireland)
ISBN 978-1-912963-08-9

Clayre Benzadón. *Liminal Zenith*
(New Poetics: USA)
ISBN 978-1-912963-11-9

Thomas Townsley. *Tangent of Ardency*
(New Poetics: USA)
ISBN 978-1-912963-15-7

Mikko Harvey & Jake Bauer. *Idaho Falls*
(Winner of James Tate Poetry Prize 2018)
ISBN 978-1-912963-02-7

John Bradley. *Spontaneous Mummification*
(Winner of James Tate Poetry Prize 2019)
ISBN 978-1-912963-13-3

Charles Kell. *Pierre Mask*
(Winner of James Tate Poetry Prize 2019)
ISBN 978-1-912963-19-5

Charles Borkhuis. *Spontaneous Combustion*
(Winner of James Tate Poetry Prize 2021)
ISBN 978-1-912963-30-0

Noah Falck and Matt McBride. *Prerecorded Weather*
(Winner of James Tate Poetry Prize 2022)
ISBN 978-1-912963-39-3

Jeffrey Cyphers Wright. *Fuel for Love*
(Winner of James Tate Poetry Prize 2023)
ISBN 978-1-912963-45-4

George Kalamaras. *That Moment of Wept*
ISBN 978-1-9995903-7-6

George Kalamaras. *Through the Silk-Heavy Rains*
ISBN 978-1-912963-28-7

George Kalamaras. *The Silence of the World Is a Fishbone*
ISBN 978-1-912963-61-4

Guillaume Apollinaire. *Ocean of Earth: Selected Poems*
Translated from French by Matthew Geden
ISBN 978-1-912963-40-9

Order our books from survisionmagazine.com

www.ingramcontent.com/pod-product-compliance
Lightning Source LLC
Chambersburg PA
CBHW061315040426
42444CB00010B/2648